THE BLACK AMERICAN JOURNEY

THE EMANCIPATION PROCLAMATION

"...On the first of January, in the year of our Lord
one thousand eight hundred and sixty-three,
all persons held as slaves within any state
or designated part of a state, the people whereof
shall then be in rebellion against the United States,
shall be then, thenceforward, and forever free..."
—The Emancipation Proclamation

BY CHARLES W. CAREY JR.

Published by The Child's World®
1980 Lookout Drive, Mankato, MN 56003-1705
800-599-READ • www.childsworld.com

CONTENT CONSULTANT
Kira Duke, Education Coordinator,
National Civil Rights Museum

PHOTOS
Cover and page 4: David Smart/Shutterstock.com
Interior: Abraham Lincoln Papers at the Library of Congress/Library of Congress,
Manuscript Division: 18; akg-images/Newscom: 25; Alexander Gardner/Library
of Congress, Prints and Photographs Division: 5, 12; Corbis/Corbis Historical via
Getty Images: 24; The Design Lab: 8; Everett Collection/Shutterstock.com: 26;
Library of Congress, Prints and Photographs Division: 9, 10, 16, 17, 21, 22, 28 (right),
31; North Wind Picture Archives: 7, 19, 27, 28 (left); Shepherd & Smith/Library of
Congress, Prints and Photographs Division: 23; Schomburg Center for Research
in Black Culture, Photographs and Prints Division, The New York Public Library:13;
Thure de Thulstrup/Library of Congress, Prints and Photographs Division: 14

LIBRARY OF CONGRESS CATALOGING-IN-PUBLICATION DATA
ISBN 9781503853683 (Reinforced Library Binding)
ISBN 9781503854086 (Portable Document Format)
ISBN 9781503854208 (Online Multi-user eBook)
LCCN: 2020943346

Printed in the United States of America

Cover and page 4 caption:
A close-up of the Emancipation
Proclamation

CONTENTS

By the President of the United States of America

A Proclamation.

Whereas, on the twenty-second day of
September, in the year of our Lord one thousand
eight hundred and sixty-two, a proclamation
was issued by the President of the United States,
containing, among other things, the following,
to wit:

"That on the first day of January, in the
"year of our Lord one thousand eight hundred
"and sixty-three, all persons held as slaves within
"any State or designated part of a State, the people
"whereof shall then be in rebellion against the
"United States, shall be then, thenceforward, and
"forever free; and the Executive Government of the
"United States, including the military, and naval

Chapter One

DID LINCOLN
FREE THE SLAVES?

Most people give President Abraham Lincoln credit for freeing enslaved people in the United States. In truth, he only freed some of those in bondage. Most gained their freedom after Lincoln's death.

Lincoln was elected president in 1860. It was a difficult period in U.S. history. White people in the Southern states lived very differently from those in the Northern states. While white Southerners enslaved people, many Northerners thought slavery was wrong. Over time, differences between the two regions of the country became serious. In December of 1860, South Carolina **seceded** from the United States. Other Southern states soon followed. This was the beginning of the U.S. Civil War.

Abraham Lincoln, pictured here in 1865, served as president during a difficult period in U.S. history.

One year after the war began, President Lincoln made the decision to free some people who were enslaved. He hoped this would help the Northern states, or the Union, win the war. In the end, Lincoln's decision led to freedom for all enslaved people in the United States.

The first Africans forced into enslavement in North America were brought to the **colony** of Virginia in 1619. The Southern economy was based on large **plantations** that grew cotton, tobacco, and other crops. These plantations depended on enslaved people for labor. Slavery never became an important part of life in the North. There, the economy centered on small farms and industry. Southerners depended as much on stolen labor as the North did on industry. Through the hard work of enslaved workers, cotton became the nation's most valuable **export**. Most white Southerners believed the Southern economy would collapse without slavery. They thought they needed free labor to sustain their way of life. Many white Southerners worried they would not be able to run their farms or support their families without enslaving people.

Abraham Lincoln was elected president in 1860 despite white Southerners' concerns about his views on slavery. His election was a major factor in the decision of those states to secede.

By 1820, 11 states had taken steps to outlaw, or **abolish**, slavery: Vermont, Pennsylvania, Massachusetts, New Hampshire, Rhode Island, Connecticut, New York, Ohio, New Jersey, Indiana, and Illinois. But that did not mean slavery was abolished completely in the North. Instead, most Northern states passed laws that gradually did away with slavery either by set deadlines or as enslaved people reached a certain age. In each of the 13 other U.S. states, slavery remained legal.

Enslaved workers pick cotton on a plantation. It was hot, back-breaking work.

Abolitionists began working to end slavery across the nation. The Declaration of Independence in 1776 stated that all men are created equal. Abolitionists believed this was true—regardless of a person's skin color. At first, many abolitionists were white and religious. But some of the most important abolitionists were formerly enslaved.

Abolitionists argued that slavery was cruel and unfair. Many Northerners began to insist that the South end slavery. Southerners grew angry that the people of the North were trying to tell them what to do. The Southern states united and threatened to secede from the United States. In 1861, that is what 11 Southern states did. Those states became known as the Confederate States of America. On April 12, 1861, the Confederate Army opened fire on Fort Sumter, a Union-held fort in South Carolina. The United States was in civil war, or a war among its own citizens.

> One-third of Southern whites owned slaves. Even so, support for slavery was widespread in the South.

Four **slave states** stayed in the Union: Delaware, Maryland, Kentucky, and Missouri. These states were called **border states** because they were located between the Northern free states and the Southern slave states. After the war began, abolitionists wanted President Lincoln to free the enslaved people in the border states. Lincoln refused. He knew the border states were important to the Union. Freeing slaves in those areas might anger enslavers there and cause them to join the South. Lincoln also had stated that he did not have the power as president to free the enslaved people in states that were not in rebellion.

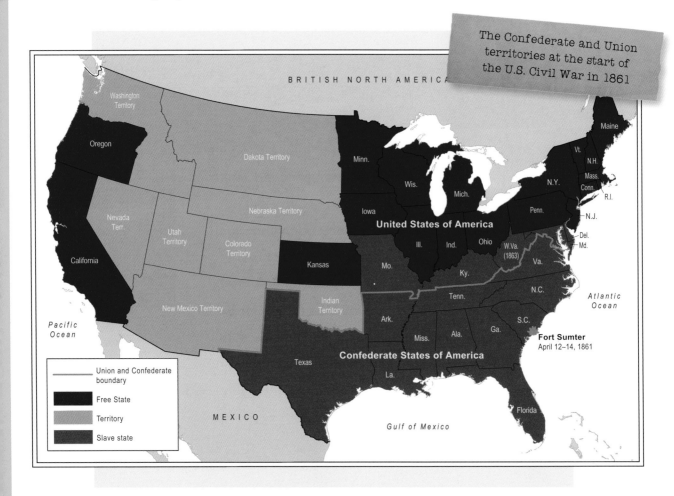

The Confederate and Union territories at the start of the U.S. Civil War in 1861

Fugitives from slavery began to look to Union soldiers for help. Lincoln told the Union army and navy not to help enslaved people escape. He wanted the South to rejoin the Union as soon as possible. If the North helped enslaved people, he thought that might never happen. In a letter to an army officer, Lincoln wrote that freeing enslaved workers would "alarm our Southern Union friends, and turn them against us."

Regardless of his personal views on slavery, Lincoln's main goal was to preserve the nation. Lincoln knew that many soldiers were not fighting to end slavery. Instead, they were fighting to put the United States back together again. Some Union soldiers did not believe enslaved people should be freed at all. Such soldiers might become angry or leave the army if Lincoln helped the slaves.

Major General Benjamin Butler

However, slavery soon became an issue in the war. In May of 1861, the Union army captured Fort Monroe in Virginia. Three people escaping slavery came to the fort. They asked the Union commander, General Benjamin Butler, if they could join his army and help fight against the South.

The Fugitive Slave Act had been in effect since 1850. It said that a fugitive from slavery must be returned to his or her enslaver. The fugitives' owner met with Butler and demanded that the enslaved people be returned. General Butler had learned that the enslaved workers had been forced to help build a Confederate fort. He did not want labor of enslaved people to be used to help the South win the war.

General Butler made a decision. He said that the Fugitive Slave Act did not apply to these individuals and that he would not return any fugitives who were used to help the South. Instead, he told their enslaver they were **contraband**.

Seven formerly enslaved men wearing their Union uniforms during the Civil War.

Lincoln was not pleased with Butler's decision. Treating formerly enslaved people as contraband meant that the Union was recognizing the seceded states as their own separate nation. Lincoln strongly opposed this idea, but he did not try to change the general's mind. Before long, other fugitives from slavery made their way to Union forces, and other generals refused to return them to their former enslavers. But when two Union generals fighting in the South began to free enslaved people in the areas their troops controlled, Lincoln asked these generals to return the fugitives.

More and more fugitives from slavery joined the Union forces. Some members of the U.S. Congress began to think that formerly enslaved people could help the Union win the war. Senator Charles Sumner from Massachusetts, Senator Benjamin Wade from Ohio, and Representative Thaddeus Stevens from Pennsylvania led the effort to let Black people join the army. All three men wanted to abolish slavery in the Confederate states and in the border states.

These leaders convinced the U.S. Congress to pass the First Confiscation Act in August of 1861. This law stated that any enslaved person forced to build forts, haul supplies, or work for the Confederate army or navy was contraband. Under this Confiscation Act, Union soldiers could help such people escape.

In July of 1862, Congress passed the Second Confiscation Act. This law stated that any enslaved person held in bondage by Confederate soldiers, sailors, or government employees were contraband as well. Union troops now could help these people escape too. The act also gave Union generals permission to let fugitives from slavery join their armies.

As the war continued, the Union army realized that escaped slaves could help make their forces stronger. Some Union generals encouraged large numbers of fugitives from slavery to join their units. General Edward Wild, who fought in North Carolina, **recruited** enough escaped slaves to form a special unit. He called it "Wild's African Brigade." Soon, he began to send Brigade soldiers to free other enslaved people in North Carolina.

Chapter Two

THE PRESIDENT CHANGES HIS MIND

President Lincoln worried about the steps Congress and the generals had taken. He did not believe that the U.S. **Constitution** gave Congress the power to end slavery. He also feared that ending slavery would anger too many white people. Lincoln worried that residents of the border states might start helping the Confederates.

President Lincoln visits with Union General George McClellan in 1862.

Public opinion was changing in the North, however. At first, white Northerners believed they were fighting to restore the United States. Lincoln had said that was the goal of the war, and slavery had little or nothing to do with the fighting. But by the middle of 1862, many Northerners supported the acts of Congress against slavery. They began to believe they really were fighting to end slavery.

Lincoln could see that many important people opposed slavery. He needed these people on his side to help the Union win the war. Lincoln also came to believe that in order to reunite the country, he first needed to address the issue of slavery. Therefore, he decided to support the actions by Congress and his generals.

Meanwhile, the countries of Great Britain and France were considering helping the Confederacy. These two countries bought most of their cotton from Southern plantations. The Union navy had created a **blockade** that kept Southern ships from transporting cotton to British and French mills. The British began building ships for the Confederate navy. The French allowed Confederate ships to raid U.S. merchant ships docked in French ports. France and Great Britain also planned to provide rifles, ammunition, and other supplies to the South.

> The Confederate army benefited from free labor, knowledge, and skills in many ways. Enslaved people were used for cooking, sewing, repairing railways, building forts, working in hospitals, and many other war-related tasks.

Abolitionists viewed President Lincoln as someone could help save enslaved people.

The site of the Battle of Antietam is now a national cemetery where nearly 5,000 people are buried. Not even 2,000 of those people were ever identified.

Lincoln was concerned that France and Great Britain would offer even more help to the Confederates. This would draw out the fighting and could lead to a Confederate victory. He knew that most citizens in those countries did not like slavery. Both countries had outlawed slavery many years before. If Lincoln could convince the British and French that the war really was about ending slavery in the United States, the two nations probably would decide to stay out of it. The North would not have to face such a strong opponent.

The U.S. Constitution gives the president special powers to use only during wartime. Lincoln used these war powers to address the issue of slavery. He decided to free only the enslaved people living in the Confederate states. This would prevent the South from using their free labor to help win the war. Furthermore, Lincoln could tell abolitionists, the British, and the French that the North was battling to end slavery. At the same time, he would not anger the citizens of the border states nor Northern states who used enslaved labor.

Lincoln first told his **cabinet** about this plan on July 22, 1862. **Secretary of State** William Seward suggested that Lincoln wait to announce his idea until after the Union army won an important battle. Otherwise, people might think the president was acting only because he was afraid of losing the war. Lincoln agreed, and so he waited.

He did not have to wait long, however. In September, a Union soldier found secret plans for a surprise attack by the Confederates. The Confederate army crossed the Potomac River into Maryland on September 17, not knowing that the Union army was waiting there for them. The battle became known as the Battle of Antietam (also known as the Battle of Sharpsburg). Although the fighting lasted only one day, it was the bloodiest battle of the Civil War. Both armies experienced more than 10,000 casualties each. At the end of the day, the Union army had won.

The Battle of Antietam ended with more U.S. casualties than any other day in U.S. military history. That includes D-Day in World War II.

On September 22, Lincoln read the Emancipation Proclamation to the public. This presidential act would free any enslaved person not living in the Union. It did not become law that day, however. Lincoln gave the South until January 1, 1863, to return to the Union. If they did not, he would sign the Emancipation Proclamation. On January 1, any enslaved person in a Confederate state would be free.

The white Southerners had the Confederate army to protect them. They decided not to release any enslaved people unless the Union army marched in and forced them to do so. Many Southern slaves were not aware of the proclamation. Millions continued to work in the South, just as they always had.

On January 1, 1863, Lincoln issued the official Emancipation Proclamation. It applied to ten Southern slave states. It did not include Northern slave states nor Tennessee, which was already under Union control.

President Lincoln signs the Emancipation Proclamation on January 1, 1863.

Chapter Three

A PRESIDENTIAL ORDER

The Emancipation Proclamation is a brief document and fills fewer than three pages in a modern-day book. Still, it is important to understand what the document says. An emancipation is the act of making someone free. A proclamation is a formal public announcement.

The Emancipation Proclamation consists of three parts. In the first part, Lincoln reminds the Confederates that he warned them three months earlier to rejoin the Union by January 1, 1863.

President Lincoln, holding a copy of the Emancipation Proclamation, is surrounded by his cabinet

The second section explains which people have been set free. The third part addresses what would happen to the freed people. The proclamation begins this way:

> *Whereas, on the twenty-second day of September, in the year of our Lord one thousand eight hundred and sixty-two, a proclamation was issued by the President of the United States, containing, among other things, the following, to wit: 'That on the first of January, in the year of our Lord one thousand eight hundred and sixty-three, all persons held as slaves within any State or designated part of a State, the people whereof shall then be in rebellion against the United States, shall be then, thenceforward, and forever free . . .*

In other words, the proclamation freed any enslaved person living in a state that still chose to **rebel** against the United States.

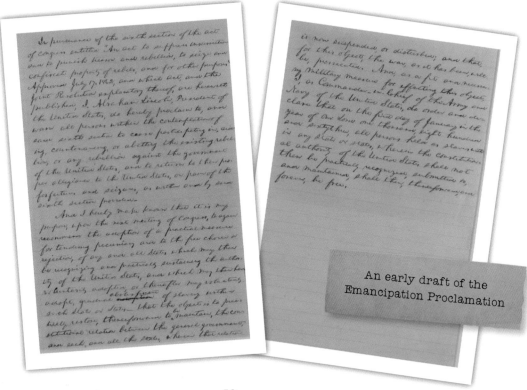

An early draft of the Emancipation Proclamation

After the Emancipation Proclamation was issued, formerly enslaved people like this group made their way North. This illustration shows freed slaves crossing Confederate lines at Newbern, North Carolina.

In the second part, Lincoln explained which states must free their slaves. The Union army had run the Confederate army out of Tennessee. The North was now in control there, so Lincoln did not free any of its enslaved people. He also did not free all of the slaves in Louisiana because the Union army had invaded only certain parts of the state. Lincoln freed only those enslaved in Confederate areas of Louisiana. The same was true for Virginia, where the Union troops had only partial control of the state.

Even after many battles, the Union did not control any part of the other eight Confederate states. These states were Arkansas, Texas, Mississippi, Alabama, Florida, Georgia, South Carolina, and North Carolina.

The original Emancipation Proclamation document is kept at the National Archives in Washington, DC. The text covers five pages and was originally tied with red and blue ribbons.

Booker T. Washington, who was seven years old at the time of the Emancipation Proclamation, described hearing the news: "We were told that we were all free, and could go when and where we pleased. My mother, who was standing by my side, leaned over and kissed her children, while tears of joy ran down her cheeks. She explained to us what it all meant, that this was the day for which she had been so long praying, but fearing that she would never live to see."

Because none of these states were under Union control, the Emancipation Proclamation went into effect. Lincoln declared that all enslaved people living in those states were now free.

The third part of the Emancipation Proclamation explained how the U.S. government would treat the freed people. The Union military would protect them and ensure that they were never returned to slavery. It also said that formerly enslaved people could join the Union army or navy.

This part of the document also discussed how freed people would survive if their former enslavers did not give them food, shelter, and clothing. Lincoln recommended that freed slaves continue to work for the people that enslaved them and insist that their enslavers pay them.

However, this was not a very practical idea. White Southerners did not believe that Lincoln had the power to free their slaves. After all, these states had seceded from the United States and did not consider Lincoln their president. The main reason the Confederate states seceded was to protect the rights of white enslavers. This meant the freed people had to make a terrible decision: attempt a dangerous escape to the North, or stay in the South and continue living and working as slaves.

Most Confederates opposed the Emancipation Proclamation, but many Northerners did not like it either. Northern enslavers feared the president might free their slaves next, while abolitionists were disappointed that Lincoln had not freed all enslaved people. Still others in the North thought that Lincoln had dealt with the problem of slavery as well as he could at the time.

Some historians argue that the Emancipation Proclamation achieved very little. It only freed enslaved people in places that the Union army did not control. How many slaves it affected depended on the success of the Union's military effort. Other historians consider the document an important turning point because it signaled the Union's commitment to ending slavery.

Formerly enslaved women continuing to work on a cotton plantation. Their male overseer watches.

Even after the Emancipation Proclamation, many enslaved people continued to work as they always had. Their enslavers refused to honor the order, and many slaves were too afraid to try to escape. And in some areas, like Texas, news of the proclamation hadn't reached enslaved people, so they didn't even know they were free. While most slaves did not benefit immediately, thousands did try to escape to the North soon after Lincoln's proclamation. As Union troops gained control of more Confederate areas, they were able to free thousands of enslaved people each day. Nearly all Southern slaves, approximately 4 million people, were freed by July of 1865.

Chapter Four

WHAT WAS ACCOMPLISHED?

The Emancipation Proclamation was not perfect. But it did achieve several important goals. First, it convinced white Northerners that soldiers were fighting not only to restore the United States but also to help free enslaved people.

People reading the Emancipation Proclamation by torchlight.

By 1863, many Northerners were tired of the war. Thousands of Union soldiers had died fighting, and the war was costing millions of dollars—meaning higher taxes. Some Northerners started to believe the Union should just let the Southern states secede. But Lincoln's proclamation made many Northerners better understand why it was important to keep fighting the war. More white people realized that slavery was cruel and unjust.

Military reaction to the Emancipation Proclamation varied widely. Some Northern soldiers were so angry that they deserted the army. Others were inspired by the idea of spreading freedom. At least one unit started using the motto, "For Union and Liberty."

The proclamation also convinced the people of Great Britain and France that the United States was serious about ending slavery. After the Emancipation Proclamation was issued, Great Britain and France offered little help to the Confederates.

The proclamation also allowed more than 200,000 Black people to join the Union forces. Nearly half were fugitives from slavery from Confederate states. Approximately 40,000 Black soldiers came from the four border states. They ran away to join the army even though they were not freed. Some Black soldiers came from other Union states and even Canada. Many of these men had been born free. Others were enslaved and had escaped to the North years before. Some joined the Union forces hoping to help free their family members and friends in the South.

Kager May is just one of the thousands of Black soldiers who fought for the Union.

These crew members were formerly enslaved. They contributed aboard the USS *Vermont* during the U.S. Civil War.

The anniversary of the Emancipation Proclamation was celebrated for more than 50 years. It is now honored on Juneteenth. This holiday commemorates June 19, 1865, the day Union soldiers brought word to Texas that all enslaved people were free—more than two years after the Proclamation was official.

The Black soldiers greatly helped strengthen the Union army. With the help of Black soldiers as cooks and laborers, more soldiers were able to fight on the front lines. The Union also formed several units with only Black soldiers.

Still, the proclamation was only in effect during the war. Abolitionists worried about what would happen to the freed slaves after the war. Abolitionists wanted to make sure those who were freed were not returned to slavery. They also wanted to extend freedom to all enslaved people.

Abolitionists began working to change the Constitution to outlaw slavery everywhere in the United States. In 1864, Congress voted on the Thirteenth **Amendment**—the amendment to end slavery throughout the United States. The House of Representatives passed it, but the Senate did not.

President Lincoln did not give up on the cause, however. When he ran for reelection later that year, he promised to push Congress to pass the Thirteenth Amendment. In the meantime, Maryland and Missouri voted to abolish slavery in their states. When Lincoln was reelected president later that year, he finally convinced Congress to approve the amendment. If enough states **ratified** it, the amendment would be added to the Constitution.

President Abraham Lincoln's Gettysburg Address in November of 1863 mentioned the Emancipation Proclamation indirectly with the phrase "new birth of freedom."

Members of Congress react in many ways after the adoption of the Thirteenth Amendment in January of 1865.

Then, on April 9, 1865, General Robert E. Lee of the Confederate army surrendered. The U.S. Civil War was over, and the North had won.

Just five days later, President Lincoln was assassinated. While many people today credit him with the end of slavery, Lincoln did not live to see the Thirteenth Amendment become law. Vice President Andrew Johnson became the next president. Johnson required the Southern states to approve the amendment before they could rejoin the Union. On December 18, 1865, Secretary of State William Seward announced the ratification of the Thirteenth Amendment. The amendment was added to the Constitution. Slavery was finally illegal throughout the United States.

Confederate General Robert E. Lee (seated at left) signs papers to surrender. Looking on are Union officers, including General Ulysses S. Grant (seated at right).

Freed slaves celebrate the abolition of slavery in Washington, DC.

The Emancipation Proclamation paved the way for a nation striving for freedoms for all. Lincoln understood how important the document was. He said, "In giving freedom to the slave, we assure freedom for the free."

**This book, as with much of history, takes a look at the
Emancipation Proclamation from a mostly white perspective.**
How might this topic have looked differently if told from an enslaved person's perspective?

**The word *contraband* is usually used to talk about goods.
Yet enslaved people were considered contraband during the Civil War.**
What does the decision to treat enslaved people like goods
(and not people) say about the system of power at that time?
Compare it to the system of slavery. How are they similar? How are they different?

TIME LINE

1610

1619
The first enslaved Africans are brought to the colonies.

1780

1789
The Constitution is ratified, containing language that sanctions slavery.

1830

ca. 1830
Abolitionists begin working to end slavery.

1833
The Slavery Abolition Act abolishes slavery in the British Empire and its colonies.

1840

1848
France abolishes slavery.

Evaluate the images in this book, especially the painting on page 13.
It shows an enslaved man appealing to President Lincoln for his freedom.
The image makes it look like Black people need white people to save them.
Who do you think was the artist of this work?
How does an image like this affect what you think about Black people?
Make an argument for or against continuing to display images like this.

Chapter Three talks about different views on the Emancipation and what it achieved.
Some people argue it achieved little as it only freed slaves in places that the Union army did not control. Others argue that it was an important turning point because it showed the Union's commitment to ending slavery. What do you think?

1860

1861
Eleven slave states leave the Union in February. They form the Confederate States of America. General Benjamin Butler decides that fugitives from slavery are contraband. The First Confiscation Act is passed by Congress.

1862
In July, Congress passes the Second Confiscation Act. Lincoln tells his cabinet about his plan to free enslaved people. Union generals free some slaves in Louisiana and North Carolina. The Battle of Antietam occurs on September 17. Lincoln reads the Emancipation Proclamation to the public on September 22. He tells the Confederates that he will sign the act into law if they do not return to the Union.

1863
Lincoln issues the Emancipation Proclamation on January 1. While the Confederate states do not recognize the order, many enslaved people take the opportunity to escape to the Northern states.

1864
Congress first votes on the Thirteenth Amendment. It does not pass.

1865
The Thirteenth Amendment passes Congress when the House approves it in January. The U.S. Civil War ends on April 9 with the surrender of General Robert E. Lee. President Lincoln is assassinated on April 14. The secretary of state announces ratification of the Thirteenth Amendment on December 18. Slavery becomes illegal in the United States.

abolish (uh-BOL-ish)
To abolish something means to end it officially. Slavery was abolished by the Thirteenth Amendment.

abolitionists (ab-uh-LISH-uh-nists)
Abolitionists are people who worked to abolish slavery before the Civil War. The abolitionists did not believe that the Emancipation Proclamation helped enough slaves.

amendment (uh-MEND-munt)
An amendment is a change that is made to a law or legal document. The Thirteenth Amendment to the Constitution made slavery illegal throughout the United States.

blockade (blok-AYD)
A blockade refers to the closing off of an area to keep people or supplies from going in or out. The Union navy created a blockade with military ships to keep Southern merchant ships from sailing.

border states (BOR-dur STAYTS)
The border states were slave states that stayed in the Union. The Emancipation Proclamation did not free enslaved people in border states.

cabinet (KAB-net)
A cabinet is a group of advisers for the head of a government. President Lincoln discussed the Emancipation Proclamation with his cabinet on July 22, 1862.

colony (KOL-uh-nee)
A colony is a territory that is governed by another country. Great Britain governed the original 13 colonies of the United States in 1619, when the first enslaved Africans in North America were brought to the Virginia colony.

Constitution (kon-stuh-TOO-shun)
The Constitution is the written document containing governmental principles by which the United States is governed. The Constitution was amended to abolish slavery.

contraband (KON-truh-band)
Goods that are brought illegally from one place to another are called contraband. During the U.S. Civil War, enslaved Black people who escaped were called contraband.

export (EKS-port)
An export is a product that is sold to another country. Cotton was a large export in the South.

fugitives (FYOO-juh-tivz)
Fugitives are people who are escaping or running away from something.

plantations (plan-TAY-shunz)
Plantations are large farms, often in the South. Plantations used the free labor of enslaved people.

ratified (RAT-uh-fyed)
If something is ratified, it is officially approved. The states ratified the Thirteenth Amendment so it could become part of the Constitution.

rebel (rih-BEL)
Rebel means to fight against a government. The Confederates chose to rebel against the United States when they withdrew from the Union.

recruit (rih-KROOT)
Recruit means to get a person to join the military or another group. The Union army and navy decided to recruit Black men to join their forces.

secede (sih-seed)
Secede means to formally withdraw from an organization, often to form another organization. The South's decision to secede from the United States led to the Civil War.

Secretary of State (SEK-ruh-tayr-ee UV STAYT)
The Secretary of State is the person in charge of relations between the United States and other countries. William Seward was the Secretary of State during the Civil War.

slave states (SLAYV stayts)
The slave states were the U.S. states where slavery was legal. The states in the South were all slave states before the Civil War.

BOOKS

Baumann, Susan K. *Black Civil War Soldiers: The 54th Massachusetts Regiment*. New York, NY: PowerKids Press, 2014.

Bolden, Tonya. *The Emancipation Proclamation: Lincoln and the Dawn of Liberty*. New York, NY: Abrams, 2013.

Meadows, James. *Slavery*. Mankato, MN: The Child's World, 2021.

Sherman, Pat. *Ben and the Emancipation Proclamation*. Grand Rapids, MI: Eerdmans Books for Young Adults, 2020.

Stanchak, John. *Civil War*. New York, NY: Dorling Kindersley, 2015.

Time for Kids. *Our Nation's Documents: The Written Words that Shaped Our Country*. Tampa, FL: Time for Kids Books, 2018.

WEBSITES

Visit our website for links about the Emancipation Proclamation:

childsworld.com/links

Note to Parents, Teachers, and Librarians: We routinely verify our Web links to make sure they are safe, active sites—so encourage your readers to check them out!

INDEX